DIRT BIKE WORLD

Enduro Racing

by Matt Doeden

Reading Consultant:
Barbara J. Fox
Reading Specialist
North Carolina State University

CAPSTONE PRESS
a capstone imprint

Blazers is published by Capstone Press,
151 Good Counsel Drive, P.O. Box 669, Mankato, Minnesota 56002.
www.capstonepub.com

♻ Books published by Capstone Press are manufactured with paper
containing at least 10 percent post-consumer waste.

Library of Congress Cataloging-in-Publication Data
Doeden, Matt.
 Enduro Racing / by Matt Doeden.
   p. cm.—(Blazers. Dirt bike world.)
 Includes bibliographical references and index.
 Summary: "Describes enduro racing including rules, course details, and stars
of the sport"—Provided by publisher.
 ISBN 978-1-4296-5021-2 (library binding)
 ISBN 978-1-4296-5632-0 (paperback)
 1. Motocross—Juvenile literature. I. Title. II. Series.
 GV1060.12.D63 2011
 796.7'56—dc22   2010004165

Editorial Credits

Mandy Robbins, editor; Tracy Davies, designer; Laura Manthe, production specialist

**Capstone Press would like to thank Ken Glaser, Director of Special Projects for the Motorcycle
Safety Foundation, in Irvine, California, for his expertise and assistance in making this book.**

Photo Credits

ABC COMMUNICATION, 5, 6, 7
Alamy/Robert Grubba, 15
Deborah Moffatt Photography, 19
Dreamstime/Pg-Images, cover, back cover
Getty Images Inc/AFP Photo/Cesar Rangel, 24; Bongarts/Christian Fischer, 13, 26
Newscom/AFP Photo/Patrick Hertzog, 23; Icon SMI/DPPI/Gregory Lenormand, 11, 12
Shutterstock/Niar, 16
Valerie Blanchette, 20, 21, 28–29
Wikimedia/Mikeldi, 9
Wikipedia/Dario Agrati, 10

Artistic Effects

Shutterstock/Irmak Akcadogan, Konstanttin, Nitipong Ballapavanich, oriontrail

Table of Contents

chapter 1

Chasing a Title

The 2009 Grand Prix of Greece had begun. Juha Salminen headed out on the long, winding course. His BMW motorcycle kicked up dirt. Salminen knew a steady pace was key on this tough two-day ride.

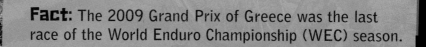

Juha Salminen

Salminen made a few mistakes the first day. But he raced better the second day. Salminen finished at the top of the **leaderboard**. The victory gave him his seventh WEC title. It was the first WEC title ever won on a BMW motorcycle.

Juha Salminen (with trophy) celebrating his victory

leaderboard—a board that displays the leaders in a competition

chapter 2

Enduro Basics

Enduro racing tests skill and **endurance**. Races last for hours. Some are spread out over several days. Enduro races run mainly **off-road**. Some also include pavement racing.

endurance—the ability to keep doing an activity for long periods of time

off-road—describes races that are run on dirt, mud, rock, or other rough surfaces

Fact: Enduro races sometimes run on public streets. Riders must have a street motorcycle license.

Enduro motorcycles have headlights and brake lights. Riders use these for racing at night or on paved streets. These bikes also have tires with deep **tread** for off-road racing.

tread

tread—a series of bumps and deep grooves on a tire

Fact: Enduro courses often wind through woods and over hills. Some courses even cross streams.

The WEC is the highest level of enduro racing. Riders travel to courses around the world. Riders can also race in the American Motorcyclist Association (AMA) National Enduro series.

enduro race in Germany

Fact: Enduro motorcycles are grouped in classes. The professional classes are based on engine power. In the WEC, classes are E1, E2, and E3.

chapter 3

Enduro Racing

An enduro race is a **timekeeping event**.
Speed is not the key to winning. Riders
travel between **checkpoints**. Their goal is
to reach each checkpoint on time.

timekeeping event —an event In which
participants must reach checkpoints in a certain time

checkpoint—one of many stations along an enduro
course at which riders are scored

Fact: Scrambles are often confused with enduro races. Scrambles are long dirt bike races, but they are not timekeeping events.

Riders take off from the starting line in groups. **Roll charts** help riders prepare for every turn on the course. Riders plan their speed to reach each checkpoint on time.

roll chart—a device riders attach to their motorcycles that tells them every turn, obstacle, and known checkpoint in a race

Riders face different kinds of checkpoints. They prepare for all of the known checkpoints. They also face secret checkpoints and emergency checkpoints. Emergency checkpoints are used to break ties.

Fact: Secret checkpoints count what minute each rider is on. Emergency checkpoints break ties by counting the minutes and the seconds.

In enduro, the rider with the fewest points wins. Riders get points for reaching checkpoints too early or too late. They also get points for breaking rules, like taking too long to make repairs.

riders leaving a checkpoint

Fact: Most championship enduro courses are 125 miles (201 kilometers) or longer.

chapter 4

Enduro Stars

Former champions like Kari Tiainen and Anders Eriksson made enduro racing popular among fans. Both men have won seven WEC titles.

Kari Tiainen

Finland's Juha Salminen is one of today's enduro stars. He has won seven WEC titles. In 2009 Salminen broke the record of 77 WEC wins.

Fact: Enduro is popular with women too. Australian Jemma Wilson and American Lacy Jones have enjoyed success in enduro.

Finland is also home to Samuli Aro. Aro has won five WEC titles in seven years. Stars like Salminen and Aro keep enduro fans coming back for more.

Fact: From 2004 to 2006, Aro won WEC titles three years in a row.

Pushing the Limits!

Glossary

checkpoint (CHEK-point)—one of many stations along an enduro course at which riders are scored, usually based on their timing

endurance (in-DUHR-uhnts)—the ability to keep doing an activity for long periods of time

leaderboard (LEE-dur-bohrd)—a board that displays the leaders in a competition

off-road (OFF-rohd)—describes races that are run on dirt, mud, rock, or other rough surfaces

roll chart (ROHL CHART)—a device riders attach to their motorcycles that tells them every turn, obstacle, and known checkpoint in a race

timekeeping event (TIME-kee-ping i-VENT)—an event in which participants must reach checkpoints in a certain time, rather than racing to be the fastest to the finish line

tread (TRED)—a series of bumps and deep grooves on a tire; tread helps tires grip surfaces

Read More

Armentrout, David. *Motorcycle Races: Motorcycle Mania.* Motorcycle Mania II. Vero Beach, Fla.: Rourke Publishing LLC, 2008.

David, Jack. *Enduro Motorcycles.* Motorcycles. Minneapolis: Bellwether Media, 2008.

Healy, Nick. *Enduro Racing.* Dirt Bikes. Mankato, Minn.: Capstone Press, 2006.

Internet Sites

FactHound offers a safe, fun way to find Internet sites related to this book. All of the sites on FactHound have been researched by our staff.

Here's all you do:

Visit *www.facthound.com*

FactHound will fetch the best sites for you!

Index